GOD HOLDS ME TIGHT

Three stories for children
based on Psalms

ELSPETH CAMPBELL MURPHY
ILLUSTRATED BY JANE E. NELSON

This Guideposts edition is published by special arrangement
with Chariot Books, David C. Cook Publishing Co.
SOMETIMES I GET LONELY
© 1981 Elspeth Campbell Murphy
SOMETIMES I HAVE TO CRY
© 1981 Elspeth Campbell Murphy
SOMETIMES I GET MAD
© 1981 Elspeth Campbell Murphy

All rights reserved. Except for brief excerpts for review purposes,
no part of this book may be reproduced or used in any form without
written permission from the publisher.
Printed in the United States of America

Guideposts®
CARMEL • NEW YORK 10512

SOMETIMES I GET LONELY
PSALM 42 FOR CHILDREN
BY ELSPETH CAMPBELL MURPHY
ILLUSTRATED BY JANE E. NELSON

"As the deer pants for streams of
 water,
so my soul pants for you, O God.
My soul thirsts for God, for the
 living God."

Psalm 42:1, 2, NIV

Do you know what I saw today, God? A deer! A real, live deer drinking at a stream of water.

She sure looked thirsty. I think she wanted a drink of water more than anything else in the world.

Do you know what she reminded me of? Me.
And the water reminded me of you.
Know why?
Because sometimes I get lonely, and lonely is an empty feeling—like being thirsty.
Sometimes I get lonely, and I need to know you're there.

I get lonely when I fight with my friend, and we're mad at each other. Then I'm afraid she'll find another best friend.

I get lonely when we go visiting, and there are only grown-ups. Grown-ups talking and talking—but not to me.

And sometimes I get lonely even when there are kids around. Like the time we went on the field trip to the museum. My partner got sick, and I had no one to be with.

But when I get lonely—you know what?—I say to myself,
Hey, why are you so sad? God still loves you. You can still talk to him.

You're my friend, God. Only you're a different kind of friend.

You're not like someone who can climb on the other side of the teeter-totter or twirl the other end of the jump rope or draw hopscotch squares on the sidewalk.

Jj Kk Ll Mm Nn Oo Pp Qq Rr Ss Tt Uu Vv Xx Yy Zz

Friday

rd   a <u>blue</u> ball

1 2 3 4 5 6 7 8 9 10

lue boat

blue
blue
blue
blue
blue

e crayon

You're a special kind of friend.
  And even though I can't see you, I know
you are with me on the playground
    and at my house
    and in my classroom
    and everywhere I go.

Sometimes I think you are calling to me. But not like my friend who calls from across the street.

It's not that I hear your voice with my ears. I hear you inside my head.

And then I feel your love all over me—
—like a waterfall splashing over the rocks.
I feel your love in the daytime.
I feel your love at night.

So those times when I get lonely—you know what?—I say to myself, *Hey, why are you so sad? God still loves you. You can still talk to him.*

And then I know you're there for me—like a stream of water
for a thirsty deer.

"Weeping may remain for a night,
but rejoicing comes in the morning."
Psalm 30:5, NIV

SOMETIMES I HAVE TO CRY
VERSES FROM THE PSALMS ON TEARS

BY ELSPETH CAMPBELL MURPHY
ILLUSTRATED BY JANE E. NELSON

You know what, God?

Sometimes I get sad and grouchy—like when I'm tired of my toys, and there's no one to play with, and I have nothing to do.

That's when I whine and cry a little.

But that's not when I feel the worst. You know what the worst feeling is, God? It's when I feel so deep-down sad that I can't stop crying.

Look at my pillow, God. It's all wet from my tears. Yesterday my dog got run over by a car. And now my crying just won't stop.

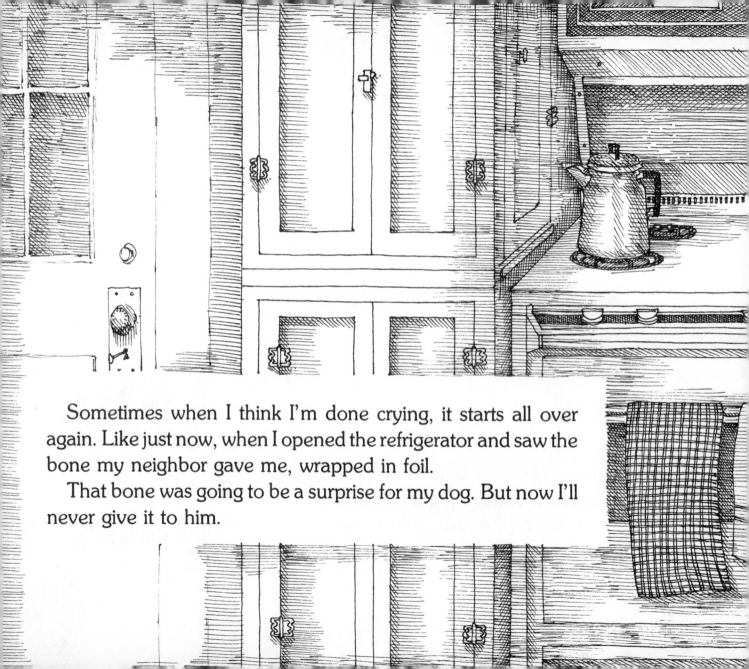

Sometimes when I think I'm done crying, it starts all over again. Like just now, when I opened the refrigerator and saw the bone my neighbor gave me, wrapped in foil.

That bone was going to be a surprise for my dog. But now I'll never give it to him.

You know, God, with all the people in the world, you must hear a lot of crying.

But you don't turn away and block up your ears. You're a good listener. And you understand.

My feelings are spread out in front of you the way we spread out papers at school. My sadness isn't hidden from you.

You know what, God? Sometimes when I'm sad, I close my eyes and pretend I'm a little baby again.

And then I imagine that you are a strong and gentle father, holding me close to you.

"There, there," I seem to hear you say. "Be still now, and just remember that I'm your God."

You let me know that it's all right to cry. And you help me know that I won't always be crying.

Remember the time I got really sick, and it seemed like I coughed all night long? That night was dark and scary—but then mom and I watched the sun come up, and everything seemed better.

Being sad is like a long, dark night, and being happy again is like the morning.

O God, you are my comforter, my
stick-beside-me friend.
How wonderful you are!

Note to parents and teachers:
The following Scriptures were
used as a basis for this story:
In order of use:
Psalm 6:8, 9
Psalm 38:9
Psalm 103:13
Psalm 46:10
Psalm 30:5
Psalm 119:76

SOMETIMES I GET MAD
PSALM 73 FOR CHILDREN

BY ELSPETH CAMPBELL MURPHY
ILLUSTRATED BY JANE E. NELSON

You know what, God? Sometimes I get mad. And getting mad is a scary feeling—like when my feet slide out from under me and I can't stop myself.

When I get mad, I need to just talk,
and talk,
and talk,
and tell you all about it.

Take last night, for example. My Great-aunt Helen has a big, old gray cat named Precious. Everyone pats him and says, "Nice kitty."

But he waited until no one was looking. . . .

Then he scratched me!
"He scratched me for no reason!" I yelled.
But everyone said, "You must have scared him.
Did you pull his tail?"

Now that's two things I hate,
hate,
hate.

I hate getting scratched. And I hate it when
no one believes me.
I'm telling you, God, sometimes I get mad.

This morning I had the swing first. But this big boy came and grabbed it and wouldn't get off. I hardly had a turn at all.

"Hey, that's not fair!" I yelled.
But the big boy just laughed and said, "So who cares about fair?"

Now that's two more things I hate,
hate,
hate.

I hate it when people grab stuff away from me.
And I hate it when they laugh at me.

When I get mad, I need to talk to you, God. Because I don't understand why people do bad things. Or why bad things have to happen.

But when I talk to you, I feel you near me, calming me down. Then I can stop worrying about bad things, because I know you'll take care of them when you're ready.

You know what, God?
When I'm fussing and fuming
and feeling sorry for myself,
I'm not really paying attention to you.

Just like my puppy won't pay attention to me when I'm trying to settle him down.

It's good for me to bring you my mixed-up feelings and tell you when I'm mad, God. Because then I remember that you're in charge, and that everything will be all right.

And that gives me a safe feeling—as if you're holding my hand to keep me from falling.